MEL BAY PRESENTS
David Barrett's Harmonica Masterclass
Classic Chicago Blues Harp #2

LEVEL 3
COMPLETE BLUES HARMONICA LESSON SERIES

CD CONTENTS

1 About the Harmonica Masterclass Lesson Series [3:29]	17 12 Bar Jam 8B [1:03]
2 Cross Harp Blues Scale [1:12]	18 12 Bar Jam 8C, Octave Substitution & Phrasing [1:26]
3 Music Example: *Blues Scale Scream* [:56]	19 High End Blow Bends &Blues Scale [1:32]
4 Music Example:*Steppin' Lightly* [:53]	20 1st Position Root Notes & 12 Bar Blues Progression [:45]
5 Quarter-tone Bends [:38]	21 Using Blow Bends for Expression [:52]
6 The Bent Vibrato [4:25]	22 Hot Licks & Blues Bits 9 [:44]
7 Tongue Blocking, Hot Licks & Blues Bits 6 [2:24]	23 12 Bar Jam 9A [:39]
8 12 Bar Jam 6A & 6B [1:17]	24 Starting in the Bent Position [:42]
9 Octave Embouchure & Exercises [1:23]	25 Hot Licks & Blues Bits 10 [:44]
10 Hot Licks & Blues Bits 7 [:38]	26 12 Bar Jam 10A [1:08]
11 12 Bar Jam 7A, 7B, & 7C [2:11]	27 Draw Harp Blues Scale [:37]
12 The Flutter Tongue [1:05]	28 3rd Position Chords & Root Notes [:50]
13 Octave Substitution [:48]	29 12 Bar Jam 11A [:38]
14 5 Hole Octave Exercises [:40]	30 12 Bar Jam 11B [:34]
15 Hot Licks & Blues Bits 8 [:55]	31 12 Bar Jam 11C [:42]
16 12 Bar Jam 8A [:35]	32 *I'm Ready*, By Willie Dixon, 3rd Position [4:02]

1 2 3 4 5 6 7 8 9 0

Visit us on the Web at www.melbay.com — E-mail us at email@melbay.com

Contents

Thanks to John Scerbo, Stu Yager, and my students for editing and proof reading.

Also, to my wife Nozomi and our family for their never-ending support.

About the Harmonica Masterclass Lesson Series

Welcome to *Harmonica Masterclass' Complete Blues Harmonica Lesson Series Level Three.* My name is David Barrett, the author of this lesson series. Although this book and CD combination can stand on its own, the studies found within the materials (Series 1 and 2) will help you tremendously in understanding the ideas talked about in this book.

The original *Classic Chicago Blues Harp Book/CD* (MB95452BCD) has been separated into two books to work within this Harmonica Masterclass Series. Due to the size of the original book, the CD did not include all of the playing examples. Having these sections separated into two books now allows us to have a complete recording for each book. The pages will start from page one, but the chapters will continue where *Classic Chicago Blues Harp Book #1* (MB99106BCD) left off. If you see a reference to section one or any chapters earlier than chapter ten, it is reffering to *Classic Chicago Blues Harp Book #1.*

Some of the background examples you might find to be a bit fast to play with at first. Use the two CD's from *Blues Harmonica Jam Tracks & Soloing Concepts #1 and #2* (MB99105BCD & MB99110BCD). Between these CD's you should find a background track that is at a comfortable tempo for you to use.

Refer to the back of this book for details about the entire *Harmonica Masterclass* series. If you have any questions regarding this book, or any other books within the line, look at the Harmonica Masterclass website at www.harmonicamasterclass.com or contact us by mail at PO Box 1723, Morgan Hill, CA 95038. Good luck and have fun!

CLASSIC CHICAGO BLUES HARP

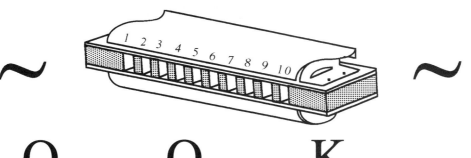

~ B O O K ~ 2

Paul Butterfield   *Photo By Lewis Campbell*

Chapter 10

TECHNIQUES FOR BLUESIER PLAYING

What Is 2nd Position?
A Deeper Look

The word Position is a term used to state the key in which you are playing your harmonica in, relative to its tuning. As we will discuss later in this book, blues uses flatted tones to get the dramatic affect it does. Because of this, harmonica players had to rethink how they played their solos to accommodate these flatted tones. In *Classic Chicago Blues Harp # 1* (MB99106BCD) we looked at the harmonica's pitch set as being constructed in four main ways: chordal, around the major scale, its octave placement, and bends. The fundamental observation about the harmonica is that all of the notes no matter what their arrangement, are based on the notes found within the major diatonic scale. As blues evolved, the harmonica player found that it was easier to play blues in a type of crossed position in which he or she acually played the harmonica in a differant key than it was tuned to. This type of playing is known as 2nd position. Even though 2nd position is not the only position that can be played on the harmonica, it is overwhelmingly the most versatile position for playing blues. To understand how positions work, we must first have a strong understanding of how blues works. Written below is the 12 bar blues progression.

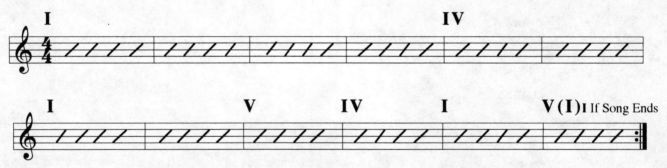

The 12 bar blues format is a twelve measure progression that is repeated until the song ends. The twelve bar blues progression utilizes three main chords: the one chord (**I**), the four chord (**IV**), and the five chord (**V**). These chords are built upon the first, fourth, and fifth degrees of the diatonic scale. The major chords have a upper case roman numeral written below them and the minor chords have lower case roman numerals written below them. Looking at the chords of the diatonic scale below, notice that the chords the blues uses are all major. Upon the **I**, **IV**, and **V** chords there are usually flat sevenths added to the chord to give it a bluesy sound. Look at the chords written below and follow the tape to get an idea of what these major chords, minor chords, and flat sevenths sound like.

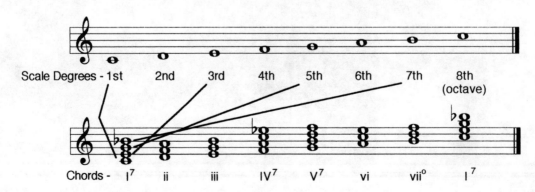

The most important observation you will need to make is how much time we spend on each chord. Each chord dictates what notes we have available to us in our solo. Looking at the **V** chord and **IV** chord in the 12 bar blues progression, there are two bars of the **V** chord and three bars of the **IV** chord. The **I** chord, known as the *Tonic*, takes seven bars of the 12 bar progression. Compared to the **IV** and **V** chord, the **I** chord takes the most importance relative to time spent on each chord. As you will see more and more as you solo, when on the **IV** chord, **I** chord licks are actually used 90% of the time. This means that soloistically the **I** chord is soloed upon ten bars out of a twelve bar progression. This finding gives tremendous importance to **I** chord style licks. Since blues uses flatted tones, which can be constructed into what is known as the blues scale, to play blues we must find a place on the harmonica where these flatted tones are available for our all important **I** chord.

1st Position

The term 1st position is used to indicate that you are <u>playing in the key to which the harmonica is tuned</u>. If you are playing in 1st position on a C harmonica, you are playing in the key of C. In 1st position the **I** chord is C - E - G. Looking at the harmonica diagram below, you can see that the **I** chord lies on the blow side.

BLOW →	C	E	G	C	E	G	C	E	G	C
	1	2	3	4	5	6	7	8	9	10
DRAW →	D	G	B	D	F	A	B	D	F	A

Without even looking any further into where the **IV** and **V** chords are found on the harmonica in 1st position, we have already run into a problem. When playing blues, bends are used to add expression and make flatted notes called **Blue Notes**. Blue notes are found within the blues scale, and are simply notes that sound bluesy when played. In 1st position, the **I** chord is found on the blows, where there are no bends available to us except on the high end. This makes blues very difficult to play in 1st position. Look at the two charts below and compare the versatility of the draw side to the blow side.

Bend Chart

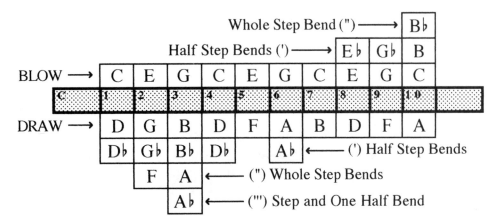

Blue Notes

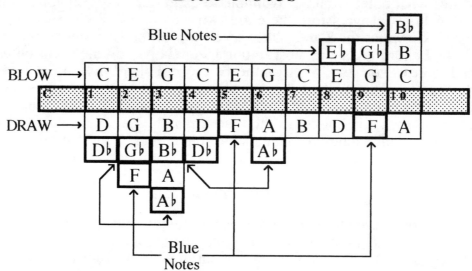

Looking at the bend chart, there are four blow bends available and eight draw bends available. The draw side has twice as many bends available to you. Looking at the blue note chart, there are three blow blue notes available and nine draw blue notes available. The draw side has triple the blue notes available to you. <u>The objective in playing blues is to make our I chord on the draw side so all the blue notes and bends are available to us at will; this is achieved by playing in what is called 2nd position.</u> When playing in 2nd position, we are actually changing the tonic to a new pitch, thus giving us a new key and scale within which to work. Instead of playing in the key of C on a C harmonica, we are going to play in the key of G. By making our central pitch G, the **I** chord (G, B, D) is now based around the draw side of our harmonica.

2nd Position

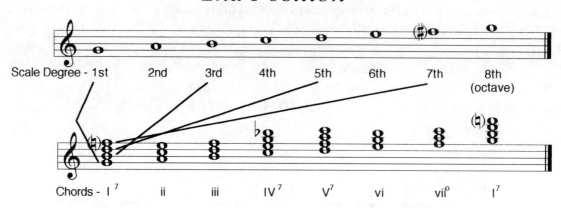

Written above is the G major scale and the chords made from it. Notice that there is a sharp in parentheses in front of the seventh scale degree, which should be F#. Because we are playing in the key of G on a C harmonica there is no F# available. In other types of music this lowered scale degree would run into problems, but in blues, it is to our advantage. As I stated before, blues uses flatted tones called blue notes. On the chords above, notice that the **I** chord has a seven notated next to it. This seven means that there is to be a note added to the chord seven notes above the root note of that chord. This seventh is then flatted, turning it into a blue note. This blue note is F natural. What all this means is that by playing in 2nd position, the key of G, you gain a blue note without having to bend the flat seventh. Let's look at where the **I**, **IV**, and **V** chords land in the key of G on our C harmonica.

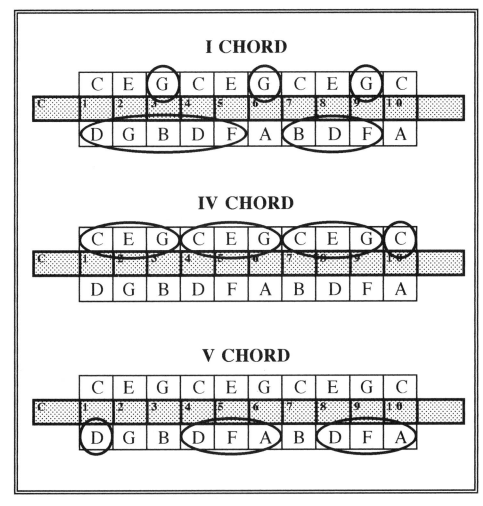

2nd Position Chords

The three chords used in blues, relative to the key of G, are notated to the left. Notice that the I chord almost takes up the whole draw side of the harmonica. The only note that is not circled is A. A, being a third above F, can also be considered part of the I chord, but for now we'll just stick to going as high as a seventh above the root. The chords discussed above are what the band is playing beneath you to support your solo. This is a very important concept that you need to understand, as a soloist, you have to work with what is thrown at you from the band. Common sense tells us that if the band dictates what we solo above, we'd better be well acquainted with what they are playing. The key to this understanding is in the blues scales.

Blues Scales

Two scales are dominant in modern music. These two scales are the major scale and minor scale. As music, and the understanding of how it works evolved, these scales were used as the underlining structure for millions of pieces of music. The blues scale, unlike many other scales, is an interesting scale in the sense that it was conceived after the music in which it was used was already known as being a discernible style. The scales that come from folk music work in just that way. Composers like Béla Bartók in the early 20th century traveled all over the world to record folk songs, later to analyze them and write their own pieces within the styles they found on the road. From these endeavors we now have such scales as the *pentatonic scale* and *minor pentatonic scale*, two scales that are very closely related to the blues scale. Unlike classical music, which is very complex in nature, blues was conceived and played from emotion, based from a history of work songs and field hollers. Just as in anything, the study of how something works usually yields some interesting conclusions, making for new ways to look at it. Many other players including myself learned their whole life by listening and mimicking other harmonica players. It wasn't until I started teaching that I discovered the importance of understanding the blues scales. The blues scales opened up a mental door that had never been there before, and because of it my playing abilities went through the roof. The blues scale isn't blues itself, but an underlining structure in which you as a soloist and songwriter can use to create blues. By the time you finish this book you will know about three blues scales available to you on the harmonica. When I talk about these three blues scales, and the overall construction of blues, there is always the traditional saying that says it's blasphemy to try to put blues in a mold; it comes from the heart and nowhere else. In some ways this is right, but for the sake of argument let's first analyze a blues song for the use of the blues scale.

Analysis of Sonny Boy Williamson's "Don't Start Me Talkin'"

Sonny Boy Williamson (aka. Rice Miller) is know for being one of the most influential bluesmen and harmonica players of all time. What I have done is taken his song "Don't Start Me Talkin'" and transcribed all of the harmonica parts and analyzed it for the use of the blues scale on each chord found in the song. I analyzed this piece with the strictest classical guidelines, and these were my findings:

TOTAL BEATS OF HARMONICA PLAYING TIME...	129 1/2 + 1/3 BEATS
TOTAL AMOUNT 0F BEATS SPENT ON THE BLUES SCALE........................	127 1/2 BEATS
TOTAL AMOUNT 0F BEATS NOT SPENT ON THE BLUES SCALE...............	2 1/3 BEATS

The time that you see not spent on the blues scale is a number that represents time in Sonny Boy Williamson's solo where there are notes that are not in the blues scale. When you analyze a piece of music and see a part that does not fit into your criteria, you look further and ask why. In the analysis of music there are decorations known as: ***Passing Tones***, where a note is used as passing to another structurally important note, and ***Neighboring Tones***, where a note is used as an upper or lower decoration (such as a two hole shake). In <u>all</u> cases where the blues scale was not used in this song, the notes were used as decoration! What did this analysis show us? It showed how tremendously important the blues scales are. Does this mean that Sonny Boy Williamson was thinking of the blues scale as he was playing this song? Probably not, but the notes fit our criteria 100%! Sonny Boy Williamson had been playing harmonica for over fifty years before he recorded this song. As a teacher, by utilizing such techniques as the blues scale, I can teach you what would normally take you twenty years, in just one; this is what the understanding of the blues scales can do for you!

The Cross Harp Blues Scale

The cross harp blues scale is very similar to a scale we already learned in *Classic Chicago Blues Harp # 1* (MB99106BCD), the cross harp scale. The cross harp scale was based on both the major scale and notes that were mostly used in blues for more up-tempo songs. Comparing the two scales below, notice the only transition you have to make between the cross harp scale and the cross harp blues scale is to lower the third scale degree (3') and add one note: the flat-five (4').

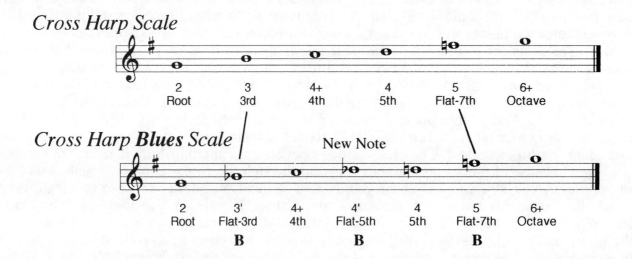

The blues scale has seven notes, of which the 3rd, 5th, and 7th are flatted. These flatted notes are known as blue notes. In the cross harp scale notice that the 7th is already flatted. As stated before, this is due to the fact that the 7th scale degree in the key of G is F#, but on the C harmonica only F is available, making for a flatted 7th scale degree. The Flat-5 is a new note added to our vocabulary. For the cross harp blues scale this Flat-5 is achieved by doing a 4 draw bend. If you look back into chapter 8 you will see that the flat-5 can be used as a passing tone or as a structurally important note, making for some nice chromatic passages. The flat-3 is still on the 3 draw, but it is bent a half step to achieve the blue note. This 3 draw half step bend is one of the bluesiest blue notes you can play on the harmonica, so work on getting that half step bend nice and tight. Written below is the full cross harp blues scale. In example 1, if a note is not available there will be an NA notated in its place, if there is an alternate note it will be written in parentheses below it. In example 2, the notes that are not available are deleted and the actual pitch name of the note is also present, take the time to memorize the notes available in each octave of your cross harp blues scale. This is the application of the harmonica's pitch set that you memorized in section 1. The **B** in bold, written below a hole number, indicates that it is a blue note.

Octave Placement For Cross Harp Blues Scale

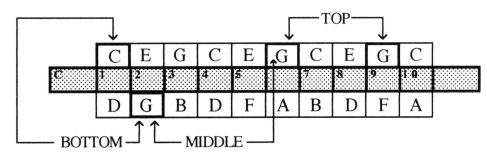

Cross Harp Blues Scales

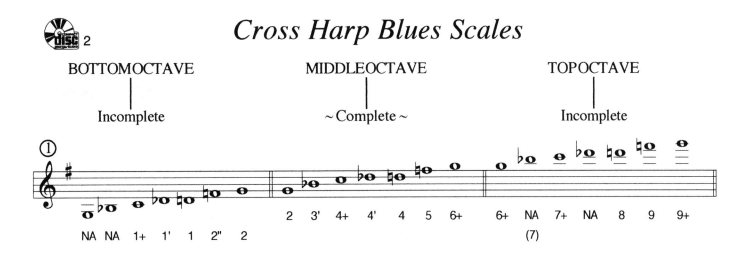

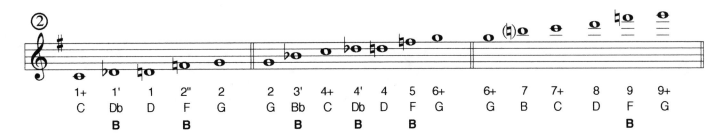

11

Lets start from the top octave and go down. The top octave cross harp blues scale starts on 9 blow and ends on 6 blow. The only blue note available is the 9 draw, which is F. Being that there is a lack of blue notes, the high end is difficult to make sound bluesy. I try to milk the one blue note available and skip over notes like the 7 draw, since it is not a blue note. The middle octave cross harp blues scale is complete with all three blue notes, starting on the 6 blow and ending on 2 draw. This octave is the most usable blues scale in 2nd position. The bottom octave cross harp blues scale has the bottom two notes missing, but is still very usable because of the vast array of bends available. So far we have looked at only one of the blues scales available to us, the cross harp blues scale based around the note G, which is used on the **I** chord in 2nd position. Just as there can be a major scale built upon every white and black key on the piano, making for the twelve keys, there are a total of twelve blue scales. As a harmonica players we're only going to study three of those blue scales. Each blues scales will be used on the I of the new key. This is known as playing in positions. You will learn about these other two blues scales as you progress through this book, but first I want to show you a couple ways of looking at your newly learned cross harp blues scale. The first thing you need to understand is that you have already been playing the cross harp blues extensively. Written below is a song that is like the songs that you played in *Classic Chicago Blues Harp # 1* (MB99106BCD). After playing the song, analyze it to see how many of the notes are from the cross harp blues scale.

Blues Scale Scream

As you can hear, "Blues Scale Scream" is very bluesy sounding. Why? because the notes it uses for its construction are from the blues scale. If you want a lighter feel in your solos use more of the notes from the cross harp scale than the cross harp blues scale. Instead of using the Flat-3, which is 3', use a natural 3 draw. Another substitution you can use is to replace your 5 draw and 2", which is the Flat-7 (F), with 2 blow and 5 blow, which is E. The example below demonstrates this technique.

Steppin' Lightly

Memorize the cross harp blues scale, this scale is the key to soloing the blues. It is a good idea to play this scale every time you pick up your harmonica to build proficiency on soloing within the scale.

5

Quarter-Tone Bends

So far in our study of bending, the smallest measurement of a bend was that of the half step. Though not apparent to most players, there are smaller degrees of the bend used called the ***Quarter-tone Bend***. Before I go into explaining how quarter-tone bends are used, we first need to review and practice all of the half step bends available to us on the harmonica. Written below is the chromatic scale available to you on the harmonica between the first and fourth hole. A chromatic scale is simply a scale that starts on a given pitch, in our case C, and goes up by half steps until it reaches its octave. Be able to play this chromatic scale both up and down with strong accuracy.

The Chromatic Scale

As we studied in *Classic Chicago Blues Harp Book # 1* (MB99106BCD) on bending, the 5 blow is E and the 5 draw is F. Since you can only bend down as far as a half step above the note on the blow reed; (being that the 5 blow is already a half step below the 5 draw), there is no half step bend available, but there is a quarter-tone bend available. The draw side transfers its vibrations to the blow side at the quarter-tone. In other words, the draw reed can only bend down a quarter-tone, then the blow reed takes over for the rest of the bend. Since the 5 blow is already a half step from 5 draw, the 5 draw will only let you go down a quarter-tone, and no further. This makes it very easy to get an accurate quarter-tone bend on the 5 draw. Listen to the tape to hear how clear a quarter-tone bend you can get on the 5 draw. Listen to, and try the example below on the quarter-tones. Standard notation of a quarter-tone is a plus (**+**) above the note head which is to recieve the quarter-tone.

Lower End Quarter-tone Bends

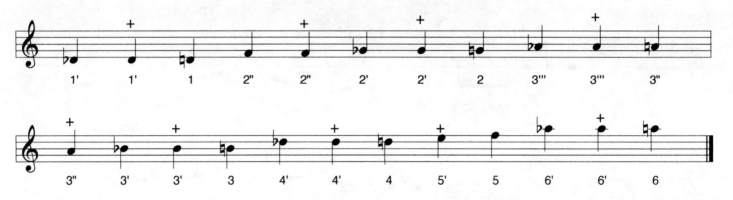

14

The quarter-tone bend will have no marking to tell you when to play it in your blues songs. When you are playing the blues, you just need to think of what type of sound you are trying to make. If you want to play more minor sounding blues, play the half step bend exactly. If you want to sound very bluesy, play the quarter-tone bend. The examples below demonstrate this. In example 1, I am going to play a lick on the 4 draw and 5 draw on a D harmonica, which makes the two notes E and G. In example two I am going to play the same notes on the A harmonica where the same notes are found on the 2 draw and the 3 draw half step bend. But where the three draw half step bend happens, I am going to play the quarter-tone instead. You will notice that example 1 will sound very minor, and example 2 will sound bluesy.

Example 1

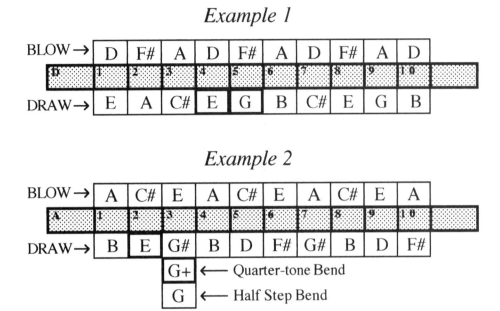

Example 2

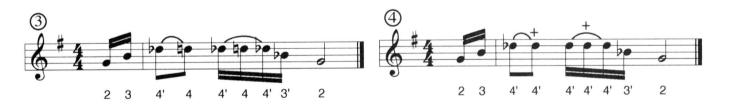

Examples 3 and 4 below demonstrates this same type of effect.

The key to playing very bluesy sounding music is in experimenting with these quarter-tones. Try experimenting with some of your favorite licks and see what different types of sounds you can create.

The Bent Vibrato

The bent vibrato is the most widely used by professional players because it has the same characteristics as a singer's vibrato. This vibrato sounds very sweet, and unlike the laughing vibrato you are actually changing the pitch of the note up and down like the waver in a singer's voice. The bent vibrato happens deeper in the throat compared to the other vibrato, and gives you a thicker tone. By utilizing the deeper part of your throat you can create a slower vibration and actually bend the note downward to create a change in pitch.

Remember back to the bending chapter when I stated that there had to be a constricted air passage to create a bend. When you are performing the bent vibrato, you are choking off the air stream, and when doing so, you are making a constricted air passage creating a rhythmic bend with your throat. When performing the bent vibrato do not try to use your tongue to bend the note. If you feel your tongue moving, find the right position in your mouth for your tongue so you can control it. The bend is actually created by the tongue, but you won't use your tongue as a muscle. I know this sounds confusing, but your tongue actually acts as a type of free moving flap that moves back and forth from the force you create with the throat pops of the vibrato. The tongue in turn creates the constricted air passage you need. This vibrato can't really be explained thoroughly enough to give it justice, so listen carefully to the tape. I feel the best way to develop your bent vibrato is to use the vibrato every time you are hanging on a note that is longer than a quarter note. Your throat vibrato might sound choked and uneven now, but with time and practice it will improve.

CHAPTER 10 REVIEW

1) The objective in playing in 2nd position is to make our _____ _____ on the draw side so all the blue notes and bends are available to us at will.

2) 2nd position on our C harmonica is based around the key of ____.

3) Write each note found in the three chords used in blues relative to G:

   I chord ___ ___ ___   **IV** chord ___ ___ ___   **V** chord ___ ___ ___

4) Write the <u>notes</u> (not hole numbers) found in the G major scale:

						F#	G

5) Write the cross harp scale from the 2 draw to the 6 blow using:

Hole Numbers -

				5	

Note Names -

				F	

6) Write the cross harp <u>blues</u> scale from the 2 draw to the 6 blow using:

Hole Numbers -

2						

Note Names -

G						

Walter Horton   *Photo used by permission. University of Mississippi Music Library/Blues Archives*

Chapter 11

TONGUE BLOCKING

There are two embouchures well known to the harmonica player: the single hole embouchure, and the tongue blocking embouchure. Both are widely used, but their applications are very different. The single hole embouchure feels very natural to most people, and is the easiest of the two embouchures to use. This embouchure just relies on the puckering of the lips to get a single hole, leaving your tongue free to execute bends. The tongue blocking embouchure utilizes both the tongue and the lips together to create a single hole (see example below). Tongue blocking opens up a vast array of techniques to you, techniques that would otherwise be impossible with just a single hole embouchure. Tongue blocking will feel awkward to you at first, but with practice, the muscle known as your tongue will become strong and versatile.

Using Tongue Blocking To Create A Single Hole

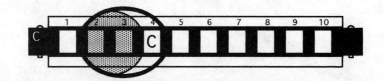

Tongue blocking is achieved by pursing your lips over three holes, blocking two holes to the left, and sounding the hole to the right. When putting your tongue on the harmonica, place the tip of your tongue on the comb wall between the two holes you intend to block, your tongue will naturally fall into place over the two holes. Think of your tongue as an articulate tool; if you just slap your tongue into place, you're likely to miss. The symbol for tongue blocking is an open circle above the note head of the note that is to be tongue blocked. As you try the exercise below, play it two ways: 1) Slide your tongue to each adjacent hole keeping your tongue rigid so it doesn't block the intended hole. 2) Reset your tongue for each hole, making sure that each hole is clean before moving on.

The Tongue Slap

The original usage of tongue blocking was to create an embouchure to play single holes. This technique quickly caught on as much more than that. When in the tongue blocking embouchure your lips are over three holes and two of those holes are blocked by your tongue. If you breathe in first and then quickly slap your tongue into position, all the air that it took to vibrate three holes is then punched through the one hole left over. The affect is a thicker sound because of the initial vibration of the three holes, and a wicked attack on the hole left over. This technique is often referred to as a ***Tongue Slap*** and is the most important reason for using a single hole tongue block. This technique takes time to learn, if your tongue slap isn't right on, your playing will sound very sloppy.

As I learned to play the harmonica this technique naturally developed from the use of tongue blocking. So practice this technique, but also understand it will come with time. Try the last exercise you just played one more time, breathing in or out before resetting your tongue for each hole to get the tongue slap.

Hot Licks & Blues Bits 6

Before you go on into "Hot Licks & Blues Bits 6", I need to talk about where tongue blocking is used and not used. For now, you will use the pucker embouchure for the first through third holes. Notes above the third hole will be tongue blocked. This is your general rule, but there are exceptions.

If you are doing a passage that includes bends, you can pucker the entire passage. If there are some notes within that passage you would like to add weight too, go ahead and tongue block them (assuming the use of the tongue slap) as long as you can switch back to a pucker embouchure when needed for the bend. You want to be careful not to make the line sound disjunct. Choose which embouchure you use carefully to make the line sound natural. Later, you will learn how to bend tongue blocked as well. This allows for smoother passages when a bend is found between tongue blocked notes. Some players eventually tongue block every note on the harmonica including their bends. Some players use a highbred style of tongue blocking in some places and puckering in others. I personally play that way.

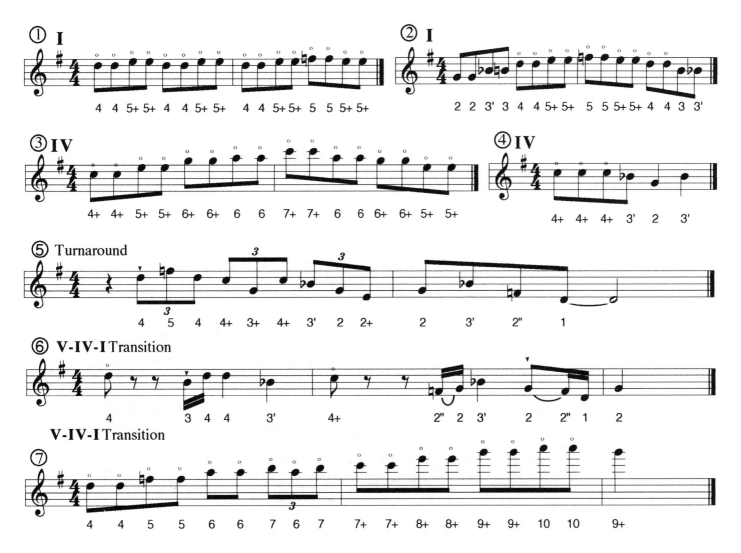

12 Bar Jam 6A

12 Bar Jam 6B

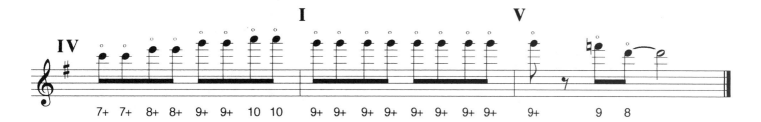

7+ 7+ 8+ 8+ 9+ 9+ 10 10   9+ 9+ 9+ 9+ 9+ 9+ 9+   9+   9   8

The Octave Embouchure

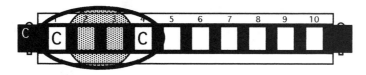

In Classic Chicago Blues Harp Book # 1 (MB99106BCD) we talked about how one of the ways to look at the harmonica's pitch set was to look at its octave placement; these octaves are achieved by tongue blocking. Tongue blocking octaves is similar to straight tongue blocking in the way that you are still blocking two holes with your tongue, but instead of sounding just the hole to the right, you are also sounding the hole to your left. Octaves are played to <u>send a broader presentation of one note</u>. When a harmonica player plays backup in a band, he or she will usually use octaves to thicken the tone of the harmonica and give it a broader sound like an organ. Looking at the note spread for the harmonica below, notice that with a four hole tongue block embouchure you can get clean octaves all the way up the blow end of the harmonica. Tongue blocking octaves can also be used on the draw end of the harmonica, but you need to change your embouchure as you go higher to accommodate the different note spread. Demonstrated below are all of the octaves available to you on the harmonica.

Blow Octave Placement Draw Octave Placement

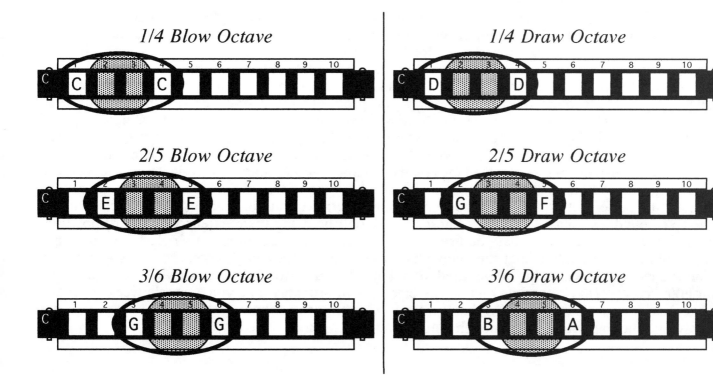

1/4 Blow Octave

2/5 Blow Octave

3/6 Blow Octave

1/4 Draw Octave

2/5 Draw Octave

3/6 Draw Octave

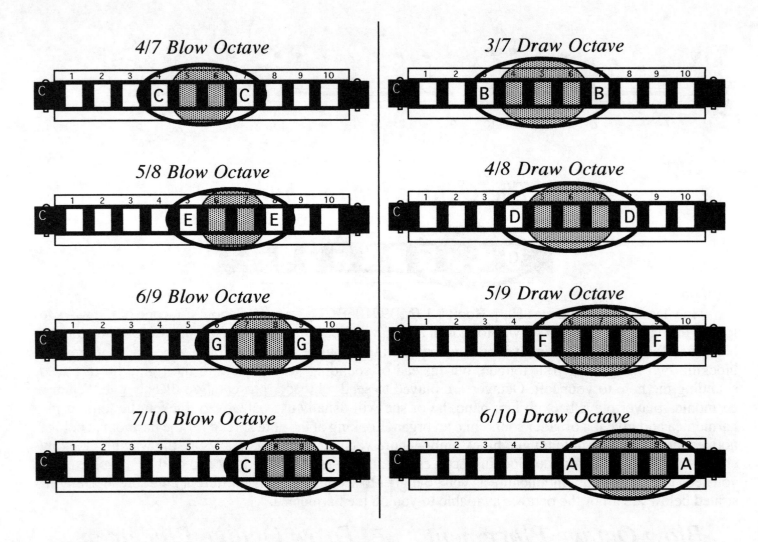

The draw side allows you one pure octave with a four hole embouchure, the 1/4 draw octave. The 2/5 and 3/6 draw octaves are actually not true octaves. Instead of the higher note being an octave above the lower, it is actually a minor seventh above the lower note. This makes for a thicker more dissonant sounding octave that can be used for building musical tension in a solo. When trying the four hole octave embouchure for the first time try to place the tip of your tongue between the two holes you are blocking on the comb wall. If you can feel the wall between the two holes, your tongue will naturally fall into place over the holes. If you proceed up the draw end with the four hole embouchure you get the same minor seventh dissonance, but at the seventh hole a new type of octave becomes available. From the seventh to tenth hole there are four pure octaves available to you by using a five hole embouchure. This five hole embouchure is difficult and takes some time to be able to use in a musical context, but the notes really scream if you hit them just right. Because you are now covering three holes with your tongue, you need to use more of the body of your tongue to necessitate the larger note spread. As you go through the next couple of songs and exercises try to get the five hole draw octaves as clean as possible; we will be using them extensively in 3rd position. Exercise 7 is the same exercise that you used to get the feel of tongue blocking single holes; the only change that has been made is that the octave has been added below each note. Exercise 4, under 5 hole octave exercises, will help you get used to making the transition between a five hole octave and a four hole octave. Take your time on this exercise. It will probably take you a couple weeks to make this exercise sound clean. If you're having trouble getting the 5 hole embouchure clean, you are probably not playing with a wide enough embouchure, so open as wide as you can.

4 Hole Octave Exercises

Hot Licks & Blues Bits 7

12 Bar Jam 7A
This 12 bar jam is an accompaniment type jam

12 Bar Jam 7B

12 Bar Jam 7C

~New Techniques~

 12

The Flutter Tongue

The flutter tongue is performed by pulling your tongue on and off the blocked holes of a standard tongue block embouchure very quickly in a stabbing (in-and-out) motion. To get the feel of this, do a slap, then another slap on the same hole, and then another—speeding this up until it's smooth. Listen to the recording for the effect this gives. This technique can be performed on a single note tongue block, or in an octave. I have notated the examples with the octave so that you can see which holes would be used. The single note flutter tongue is the most common. The notation for a flutter tongue uses the same notation we use for the shake, but in this case the three slashes are placed between the two note heads of the octave. As a side note, some players also do this technique where they move their tongue side-to-side (left-to-right). This gives an interesting effect. Try both to see which one feels and sounds best to you.

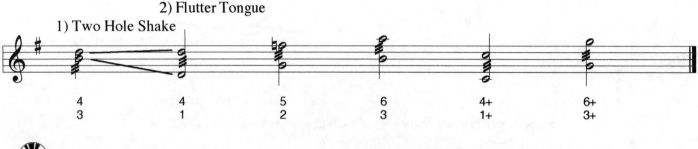

 13

Octave Substitution

Octave substitution is simply the act of taking a lick or phrase from one octave and transferring it to another octave. One of the techniques in which we're going to use octave substitution is to transfer licks from the low end of our harmonica, where most people feel comfortable soloing, to the high end, where most people are not comfortable soloing. This technique is what helped me in becoming fluent on the high end of my harmonica. There are some small differences between the high end cross harp blues scale and the middle cross harp blues scale. Let's study the differences so that we can make some generalizations about moving licks back and forth. Written below is the high end cross harp blues scale and the middle cross harp blues scale.

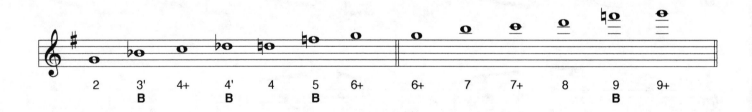

The middle cross harp blues scale is complete. The high end cross harp blues scale is missing the Flat-3 and the flat-5. These missing notes, being blue notes, make bluesy playing on the high end of our harmonica difficult; but if we're careful and clever, we can work around these missing notes. The diagram below demonstrates the note relations of the high end to the low end.

High -	G	B	C		D	F	G	-	6+	7	7+	8	9	9+
Middle -	G	Bb	C	Db	D	F	G	-	2	3'	4+	4'	4	5	6+

The 3rd scale degree (7 draw) on the high end is available, but it's natural instead of flatted; in other words, the lowered blue note is not available. When transferring licks to the high end, make sure that the licks you transfer use an unbent 3 draw. The Flat-5 is also not available on the high end, so when transferring licks to the high end don't use licks that use the 4 draw half step bend (Db). All-in-all, using octave substitution on the cross harp blues scale is very easy. The examples below demonstrate this octave substitution technique. The last example in this chapter (12 Bar Jam 8C) demonstrates octave substitution in conjunction with phrasing.

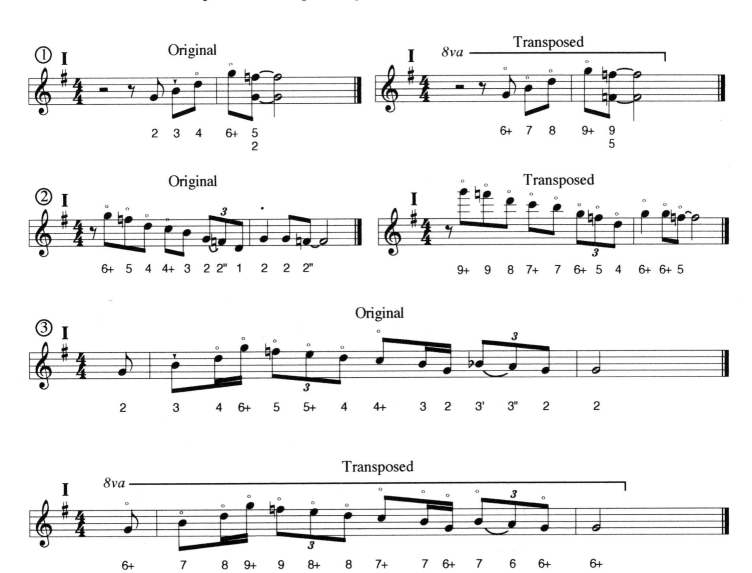

5 Hole Octave Exercises

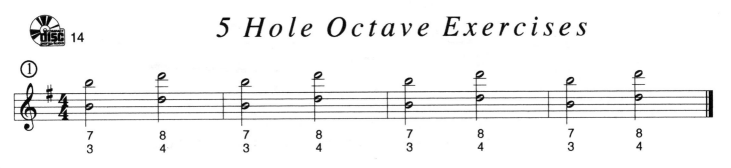

Hot Licks & Blues Bits 8

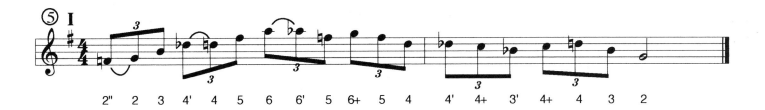

2" 2 3 4' 4 5 6 6' 5 6+ 5 4 4' 4+ 3' 4+ 4 3 2

Ending

9+ 9+ 9 8 7+ 6 6' 6+ 5 4 4' 4+ 3' 2 2" 1 3' 3" 2 2

 16

12 Bar Jam 8A

This is a 3rd position type song. We will study the structure of this song in greater detail when we get into 3rd position.
(Notes sound one octave higher than written)

© 2004 BY MEL BAY PUBLICATIONS,INC., PACIFIC, MO 63069. ALL RIGHTS RESERVED.

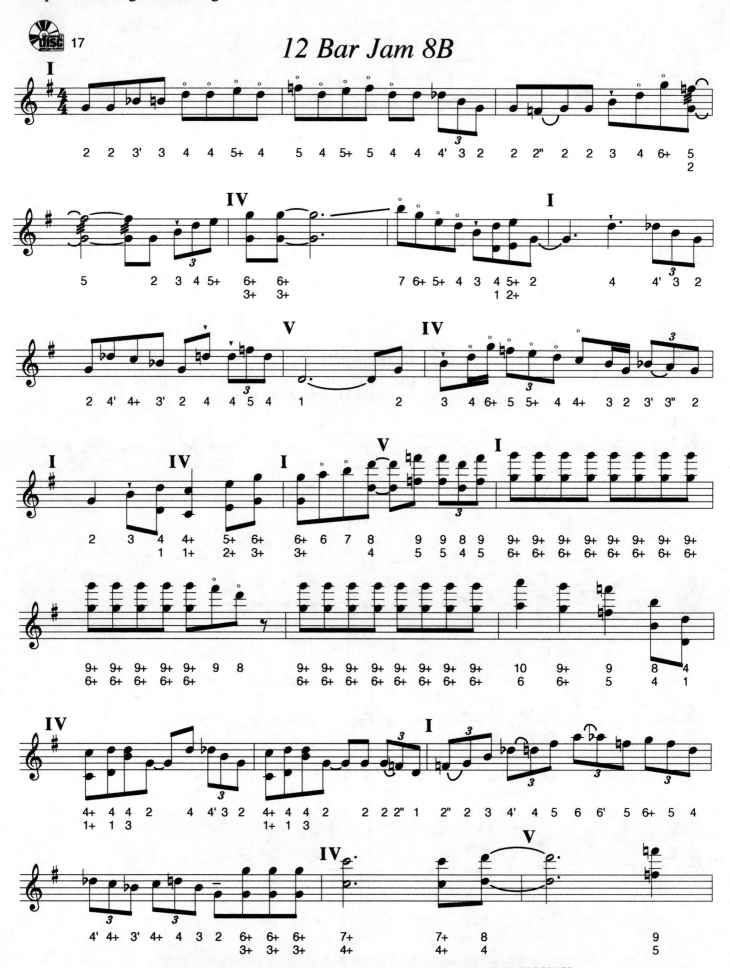

12 Bar Jam 8B

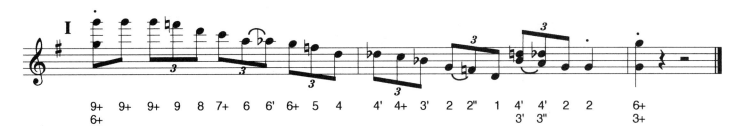

Octave Substitution & Phrasing (12 Bar Jam 8C)

Chapter 12

BLOW BENDS & 1ST POSITION

Many people find the high end of their harmonica to be a mysterious place. In many ways it is mysterious, and to some extent very frustrating at first to understand. At the 7th hole, the harmonica does a kind of back flip. All of the holes from the 1st to the 6th have the draw reeds higher than the blow reeds. At the 7th hole it switches to having the blow reeds higher than the draw reeds, making for some interesting changes in soloing patterns, octaves, and bends. To better understand the high end, let's study these differences and the effect they have on our soloing. Written below are the upper and lower cross harp scales.

Upper & Lower Cross Harp Scale

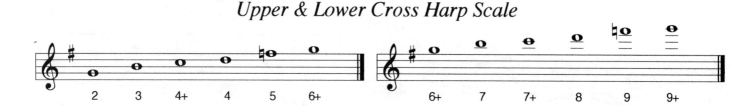

2	3	4+	4	5	6+

6+	7	7+	8	9	9+

The upper cross harp scale is an exact duplicate of the lower cross harp scale at the octave, but there is some differences in the hole pattern. Between the lower and upper octaves the draws and blows are exactly the same, with exception to the first note in the upper cross harp scale. In other words: the second note in the scale (B) is a draw on the low end and high end, the third note in the scale (C) is a blow on the low end and high end, the fourth note in the scale (D) is a draw on the low end and high end, the fifth note in the scale (F) is a draw on the low end and high end, the sixth note in the scale (G) is a blow on the low end and high end. What brings confusion in soloing is, when on the lower octave, to get the next note you would move up or down and then draw; in the upper octave, to get the next note, in two occasions you just draw on the same hole. The diagrams below demonstrate this note placement.

Upper & Lower Cross Harp Scale Placement

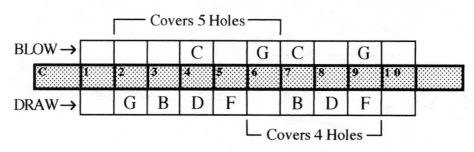

Octave & Flat 7

3rd & 4th Scale Degree

Written below is the same song played in two ways: the first song uses the lower cross harp scale and the second is one octave higher using the upper octave cross harp scale.

Example 1 & 2, Upper & Lower Cross Harp Scale

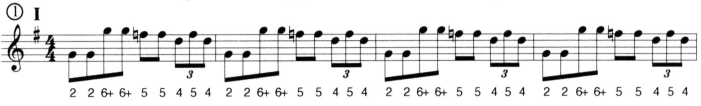

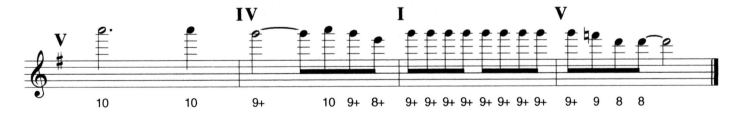

High End Bends

Because of the shift that happens at the high end of the harmonica, bending drastically changes. In chapter 6 we saw that when doing a bend the draw reed vibrates and bends <u>down</u> a quarter-tone and then transfers its vibration to the blow side. On the high end, since the blows are higher than the draws, there is no blow reed for the draw reed to transfer its vibrations to. The high end does not accommodate draw bending but it does accommodate blow bending. The same manipulations happen during the bend, but the blow reed now transfers its vibrations to the lower draw reed. The diagram below shows the transition that happens between the blow side and draw side during a blow bend.

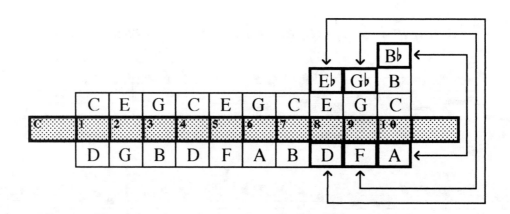

Looking at the 7 blow and 7 draw, there is no half step between them, so there is no bend possible. The 8 blow and 8 draw are separated by half step, so the half step bend (E-flat) is available. The 9 blow and 9 draw are separated by half step, so the half step bend G-flat is available. The 10 blow and 10 draw are separated by a whole step, so the half step bend (B) is available, and the whole step bend (B-flat) is available. Written below is the complete bend chart for your 10 hole diatonic harmonica.

Bend Chart

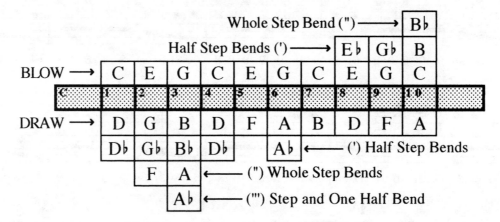

Blow Bending

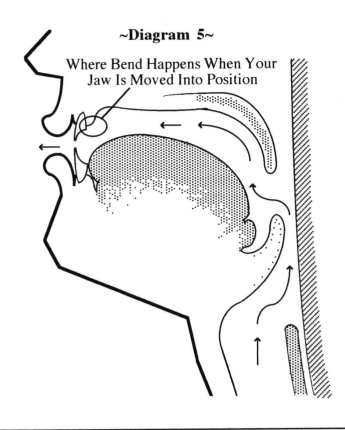

~Diagram 5~

Where Bend Happens When Your Jaw Is Moved Into Position

The first thing that needs to be considered about blow bends is what key of harmonica you're using. When doing blow bends, the key of harmonica should be a C or below; anything above a C, the reeds are too short and stiff to bend. Looking at the diagram, notice how far your tongue is in the front of your mouth in relation to the other bending embouchures. Since the reeds are so short and stiff on the high end, it takes a strong rigid embouchure to get a bend. For a blow bend, the tip of your tongue should curl behind the front part of your bottom set of teeth. While performing a blow bend, your tongue stays stiff and rigid, your jaw is what moves up and down to create the bend. By doing this, you have complete strength and control for the bend. When first trying a blow bend, put your tongue in position behind your teeth and with a high amount of pressure hiss like a snake through the hole. Don't worry about blowing to hard, the high end bends need a lot of pressure.

Blow Bend Exercises

19

35

1st Position

The blow bends we just covered give us the same type of versatility based off C, as the low end gives us based around G. These blow bends now make 1st position type playing more versatile in blues. Written below is the straight harp blues scale. In example 1, if a note is not available there will be an NA notated in its place; the actual pitch names are notated below the harmonica tab. Take the time to memorize the notes available in each octave of your straight harp blues scale; this is the application of the harmonica's pitch set that you memorized in section 1. In example 2, the notes that are not available are deleted and their substitutions are present. The **B** in bold, written below a hole number, indicates that it is a blue note.

Octave Placement For Straight Harp

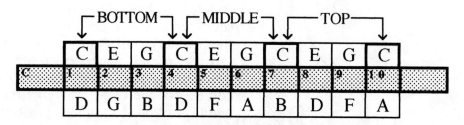

Straight Harp Blues Scales

Looking at example 2 you'll notice that the middle octave has been deleted. As you can see in example 1 there are no blue notes available, thus no blues scale on that part of our harmonica is available. This leaves us with two octaves: the upper octave, which is complete, and the lower octave which is only missing one blue note, the Flat-3.

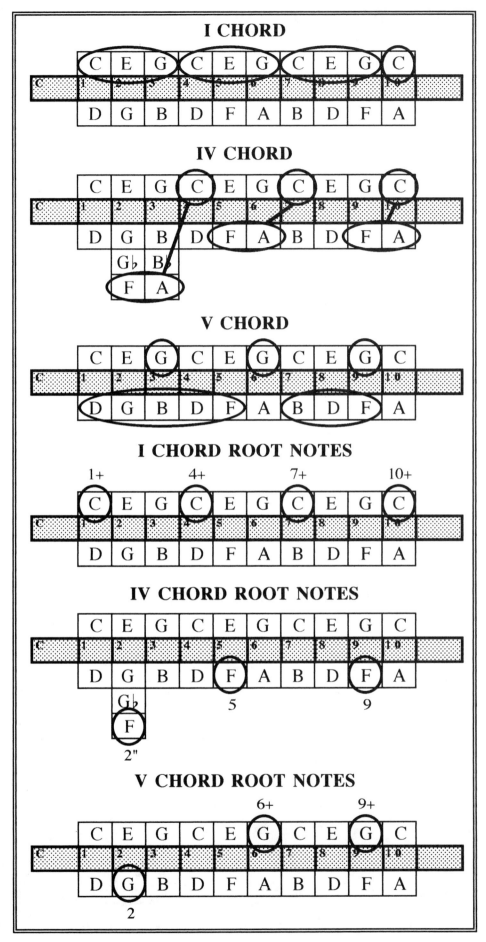

I CHORD

IV CHORD

V CHORD

I CHORD ROOT NOTES

IV CHORD ROOT NOTES

V CHORD ROOT NOTES

1st Position Chords

The same chords and patterns we used in 2nd position for blues are exactly the same in 1st position, only the notes change. The **I** chord relative to C is C - E - G - Bb, the **IV** chord relative to C is F-A-C, and the **V** chord relative to C is G-B-D-F. The chord placement for each of these chords are shown to your left. As you can see, each chord is very complete on our harmonica. The only chord that gets a little difficult to use is the **IV** chord, but when on the **IV** chord, soloistically you are using **I** chord type licks anyway. In 2nd position, the root notes of each chord were the starting place in our soloing, so in 1st position the root notes are also going to be our starting place. You will find that playing in positions is almost as simple as knowing where your chords are relative to each key. Written on the next page are two exercises that use these 1st position root notes. Exercise 1 uses the lower octave and exercise 2 uses the upper octave. One chord we want to pay special attention to is the **V** chord. The **V** chord in 1st position is the same as the **I** chord in 2nd position. This means that when on the **V** chord in 1st position you can use all of the lick vocabulary you have already learned in 2nd, which makes getting used to soloing in 1st position easier. Another observation brings up the fact that the **I** chord in 1st position was the **IV** chord in 2nd. This observation isn't as profound because we never really use the **IV** chord as a heavy soloistic place in the blues.

1st Position 12 Bar Blues Root Notes
Exercise 1

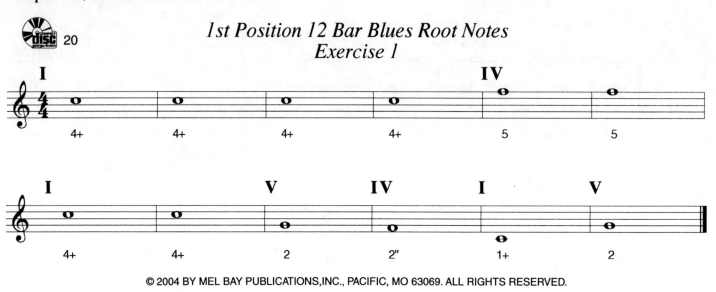

Exercise 2

Using Blow Bends For Expression

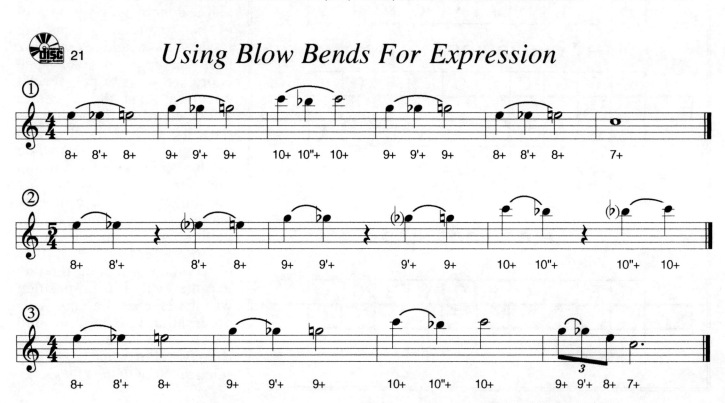

Hot Licks & Blues Bits 9

12 Bar Jam 9A

Chapter 13

3RD POSITION & OTHER EXTENDED POSITIONS

Where Positions Got Their Name

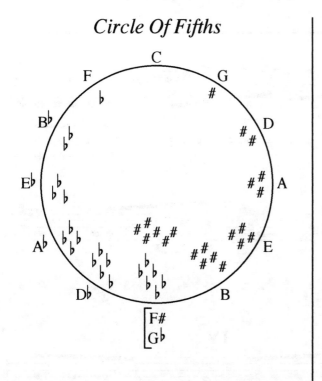

Circle Of Fifths

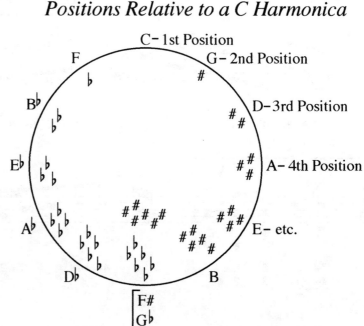

Positions Relative to a C Harmonica

The circle of fifths is a reference chart showing how many sharps or flats a particular key has. As you start from the top and go around clockwise the number of sharps increases and then at the bottom the sharps start enharmonically changing to flats. The word *enharmonic* is a term used to say that one pitch can be named in two ways. Looking at the chart below, notice that when going down from a white key to the black key you get its flat (ex. B - Bb, A - Ab, G - Gb, etc.). Also notice that as you go up from a white key to a black key you get its sharp (ex. A - A#, G - G#, etc.). As an example look at the note C#/Db. If you go up a half step from C you get C#. If you go down a half step from D you get Db. Notice that C# and Db are the same pitch; this is what is meant by the term enharmonic. When there is a choice between two names, your context will tell you which one to use. As you go clockwise and get to the bottom of the chart, it is easier to notationally switch to a key signature with flats.

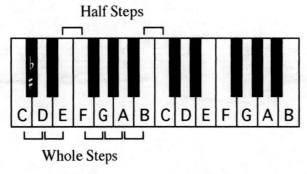

42

As for the origin of the name of the position, it comes from this circle of fifths. At the top is the key of C with no sharps or flats, this is 1st position. As you go clockwise you next get the key of G, which has one sharp (F#); this is 2nd position. The next key is the key of D, which has two sharps, this is 3rd position. To get all of the other positions you just keep on going clockwise to the key of F, which is 12th position. The key to understanding positions is to realize that you are trying to play a C harmonica in other keys. Since the C harmonica has no flats or sharps you need to watch your step with keys that have too many flats or sharps. There is a criteria that I follow when judging the validity of a position. The check list below is what we are going to use to judge all twelve of the positions.

Position Criteria

I Chord Criteria

1) Is the **I** chord available? *The **I** chord, being the most soloistically most important chord, must be available to solo within the blues.*
2) Is the **I** chord available on the harmonica's natural pitch set? *Just because you have the **I** chord available doesn't mean that it's easy to play. As we will see in studying each position, sometimes the **I** chord is only available by bending, making smooth soloing and crisp notes difficult. Having the **I** chord available on the harmonica's natural draws and blows makes for faster, more articulate, cleaner sounding soloing patterns.*
3) Are bends available on the **I** chord? *Bending makes available to us notes on our harmonica that would otherwise be impossible. The blue notes found within the blues scale are for the most part made available from bending, so having bends on our most important chord, the **I** chord, is very important for bluesy type soloing.*
4) Is there a blues scale available on the **I** chord? *The blues scale, being based from blues itself, is structurally important for soloing.*
5) Is the mixolidian scale available on **I** chord? *This last criteria for the **I** chord is for the option of light playing. When playing deep blues, you're mostly using the blues scale for the construction of your solos; when playing light or more up tempo blues, the notes you will be using for your solos are mostly based around the mixolidian scale. The mixolidian scale is just like the major scale, but its 7th scale degree is lowered.*

IV & V Chord Criteria

1) Are the **IV** chord and **V** chord available? Since there is more than just the **I** chord in blues, we must also consider the **IV** chord and **V** chord. Soloistically, the same rules of availability apply to the V chord; the IV chord, usually being not as soloistically important, only the root note is really needed for soloing.
2) Are the **IV** chord and **V** chord available on the harmonica's natural pitch set? Again, soloing is made easier when notes are available on the harmonica's natural note spread.
3) Are there bends available on the **IV** chord and **V** chord? Again, you need bends available to play bluesy.
4) Is there a blues scale available on the **V** chord? A blues scale on the **IV** chord is not usually used, but on the **V** chord a blues scale is used.

1st Position Soloing

As we go through each position on the harmonica we're going to use this criteria I set forth. To start off, lets look at 1st position and go down the list.

1st position is based around the key of C major on a C harmonica. When playing in 1st position on a C harmonica, <u>you are playing in the key of C</u>.

1st Position C Major Scale

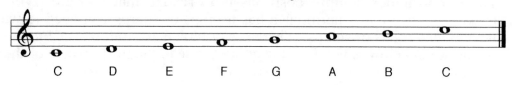

C   D   E   F   G   A   B   C

#1) Is the **I** chord available? *Yes*
#2) Is the **I** chord available on the harmonica's natural pitch set? *Yes*

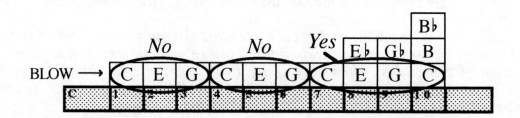

#3) Are bends available on the **I** chord? *Only the 7 through 10 has bends available, making strong bluesy playing only available on the high end. Blues is known for its dark and rich sound making for most of the soloing on the low end of the harmonica. When playing on the high end in 1st position, expect it to stand out.*

#4) Is there a blues scale available on the **I** chord? *The bottom octave straight harp blues scale is only missing one note, but soloing is made difficult because of all the articulate bends that it demands; this makes for smooth soloing on the low end fairly difficult. The top octave straight harp blues scale is complete, but as stated before, the high pitch also makes overall bluesy playing difficult.*

Straight Harp Blues Scales

BOTTOM OCTAVE	MIDDLE OCTAVE	TOP OCTAVE
Incomplete	<u>Not Available</u>	~ Complete ~

1+	NA	2"	2'	2	3'	4+	4+	NA	5	NA	6+	NA	7+	7+	8'+	9	9'+	9+	10"+	10+
C	Eb	F	Gb	G	Bb	C	C	Eb	F	Gb	G	Bb	C	C	Eb	F	Gb	G	Bb	C

#5) Is the mixolidian scale available on **I** chord? *Yes*

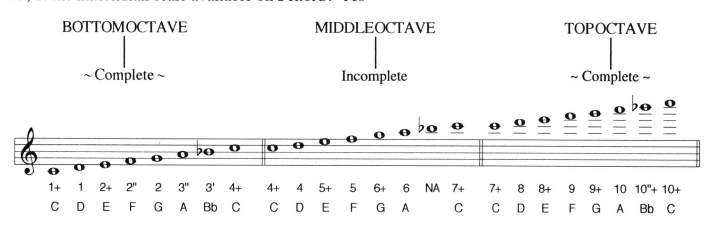

#1) Are the **IV** chord and **V** chord available? *Yes*
#2) Are the **IV** chord and **V** chord available on the harmonica's natural pitch set? *Mostly*

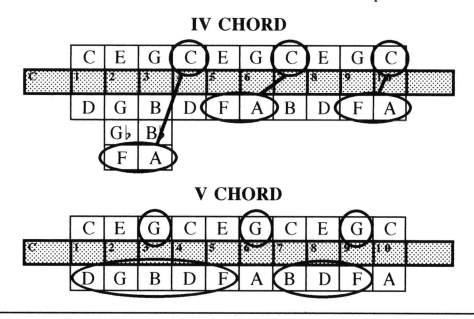

#3) Are there bends available on the **IV** chord and **V** chord? *As you can see, the V chord has a wide variety of bends available on it, but the IV chord's bends are very scarce. But again, no problem, we'll just rely on the I chord.*

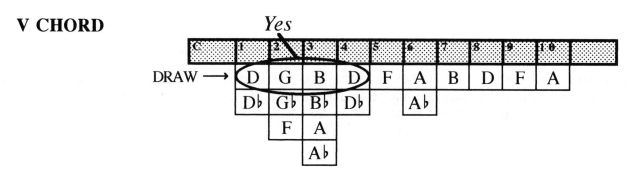

IV CHORD

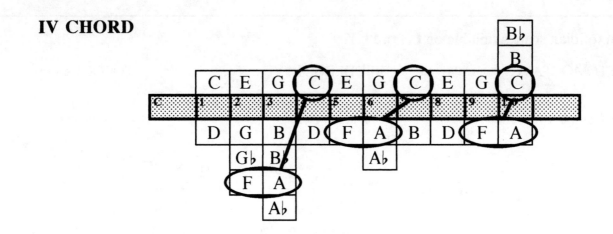

#4) Is there a blues scale available on the **V** chord? *Yes.*

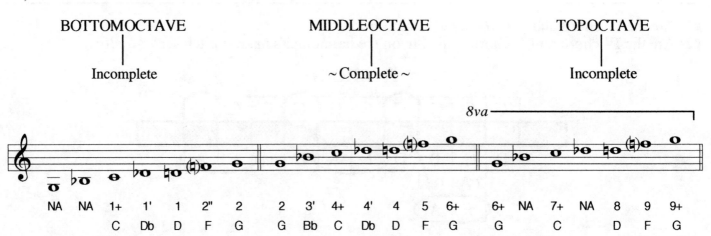

BOTTOMOCTAVE	MIDDLEOCTAVE	TOPOCTAVE
Incomplete	~ Complete ~	Incomplete

NA	NA	1+	1'	1	2"	2	2	3'	4+	4'	4	5	6+	6+	NA	7+	NA	8	9	9+
		C	Db	D	F	G	G	Bb	C	Db	D	F	G	G		C		D	F	G

1st Position Generalizations

Overall, 1st position passes most of the criteria. The only problems I have are with the **I** chord. The bottom straight harp blues scale is tough to solo upon smoothly and the top octave straight harp blues scale is available, but the bends are very articulate and take much time to learn how to play smoothly. The other problem is that the octave with the complete blues scale is so high that deep blues is difficult to play. Don't dismiss 1st position because of this! The whole reason behind playing in different positions is to make soloing material available to us that aren't available in others. As you have seen in chapter 12, there are some nice solos you can do in 1st position, so keep an open mind.

2nd Position Soloing

2nd position is based around the key of G major on a C harmonica. G major is the 2nd key to the right in the circle of fifths, thus the name 2nd position. As you will see, 2nd position is the most usable, and most used position on the harmonica for country and blues. When playing in 2nd position on a C harmonica, <u>you are playing in the key of G</u>.

2nd Position G Major Scale

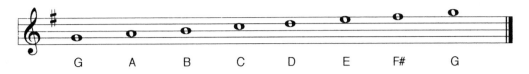

G   A   B   C   D   E   F#   G

#1) Is the I chord available? *Yes. Take notice that the I chord in 2nd position is the same as the V chord in 1st. As you switch from 1st position to 2nd position, you can use the same licks that you used on the V chord in 1st, on the I chord in 2nd.*

#2) Is the I chord available on the harmonica's natural pitch set? *Yes*

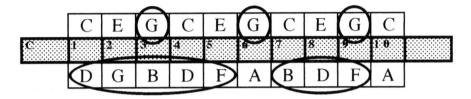

#3) Are bends available on the I chord?

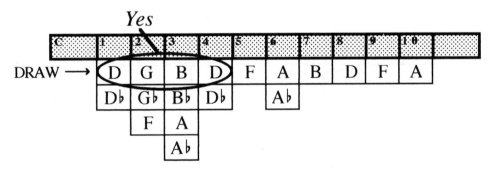

#4) Is there a blues scale available on the I chord? *Yes. As we mentioned in chapter 10, the cross harp blues scale, based off of G, is the best blues scale available on our harmonica for soloing. Having all of the chord tones on the natural pitch set, plus having bends available on all these chord tones makes for a power packed I chord in 2nd position.*

Cross Harp Blues Scale

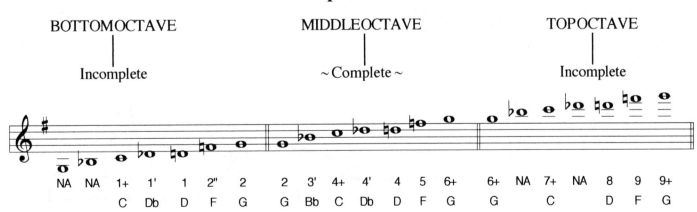

47

#5) Is the mixolidian scale available on **I** chord? *Yes*

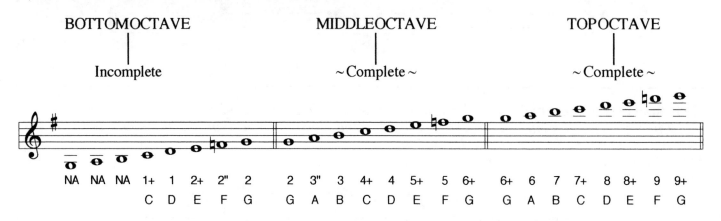

	BOTTOM OCTAVE				MIDDLE OCTAVE				TOP OCTAVE		
	Incomplete				~ Complete ~				~ Complete ~		

NA NA NA 1+ 1 2+ 2" 2 2 3" 3 4+ 4 5+ 5 6+ 6+ 6 7 7+ 8 8+ 9 9+
C D E F G G A B C D E F G G A B C D E F G

#1) Are the **IV** chord and **V** chord available? *Yes, but the **V** chord's third is lowered making for a very minor sounding **V** chord.*

#2) Are the **IV** chord and **V** chord available on the harmonica's natural pitch set? *Yes*

IV CHORD

V CHORD

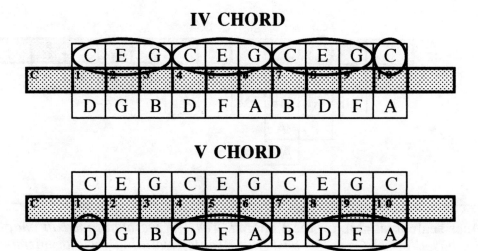

#3) Are there bends available on the **IV** chord and **V** chord? *As you can see, the **V** chord has a wide variety of bends available on it, but the **IV** chord's bends are very scarce except for the high end; But again, no problem, we'll just rely on the **I** chord. The **V** chord in 2nd position is spelled D, F#, A, but the F# is not included in the diagram. In the blues scale the third is lowered for bluesy playing, so there is no problem with having the F# missing. Also take notice that the **IV** chord in 2nd position is the same as the **I** chord in 1st. You will notice many correlations between positions before we are finished.*

IV CHORD

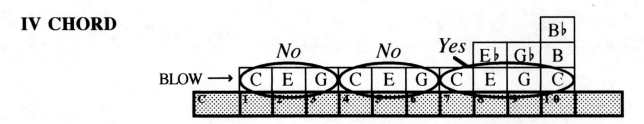

V CHORD

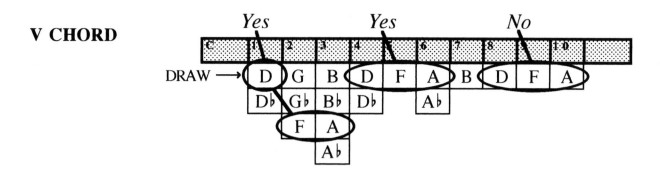

___

#4) Is there a blues scale available on the **V** chord? *Yes. The blues scale written below is based on the note D on a C harmonica and is known as the **draw harp blues scale**. The bottom and middle octaves are complete with the top octave only missing two notes. One of the first things that hit me when I discovered this blues scale was that it was more complete than the cross harp blues scale, supposedly the best blues scale available on our harmonica. After I had some time to develop soloing on this draw harp blues scale I found that just having the presence of the blues scale wasn't enough, other soloistic things needed to be available. As we go into 3rd position I will discuss these findings, for now let's accept that this draw harp blues scale makes for a fabulous blues scale on the V chord in 2nd position.*

Draw Harp Blues Scale

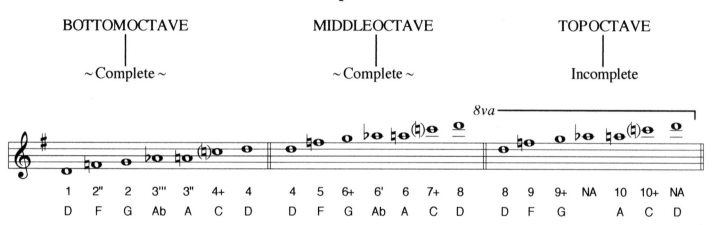

2nd Position Generalizations

2nd position is definitely the best position to be soloing in. All of the chord tones for each chord Are available on the natural pitch set, and to some degree, each chord tone has a bend on it. In addition to this, there is a blues scale available on each chord: the cross harp blues scale on the **I** chord (G), the straight harp blues scale on the **IV** chord (C), and the draw harp blues scale on the **V** chord (D). In combination with the blues scale I also found it to be very important to have the mixolidian scale available on the **I** chord. Artist will either use the mixolidian scale just for light playing, or they will switch back and forth between the blues scale and the mixolidian scale for contrast. I want to make sure to state one thing before we move on to other positions, 2nd position is used most frequently; about 95% of the time, only 5% of the time do artists use other positions. Learn each position thoroughly, but I recommend putting most of your emphasis on the harmonica in 2nd position, as most of this book has already done.

3rd Position

3rd position is based around the key of D major on a C harmonica. D major is the 3rd key to the right in the circle of fifths, thus the name 3rd position. When playing in 3rd position on a G harmonica, <u>you are playing in the key of D</u>.

3rd Position D Major Scale

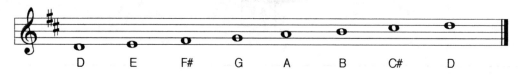

D   E   F#   G   A   B   C#   D

#1) Is the **I** chord available? *Yes*

#2) Is the **I** chord available on the harmonica's natural pitch set? *Yes, but notice; to get the third you must bend the 2 draw down a half step and the 9 blow down a half step to get the F# (enharmonic Gb). The option taken by most players is to restrict 3rd position playing to very minor, or bluesy sounding songs instead of trying to use it for light playing, which is fairly difficult.*

#3) Are bends available on the **I** chord? *Yes, but are fairly difficult on upper and lower octaves.*

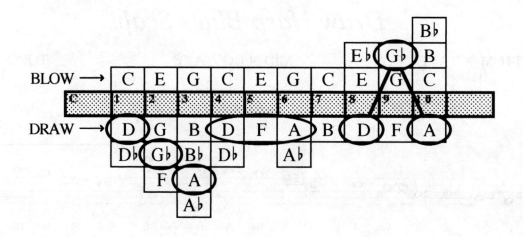

#4) Is there a blues scale available on the **I** chord? *Yes, very complete.*

Draw Harp Blues Scales

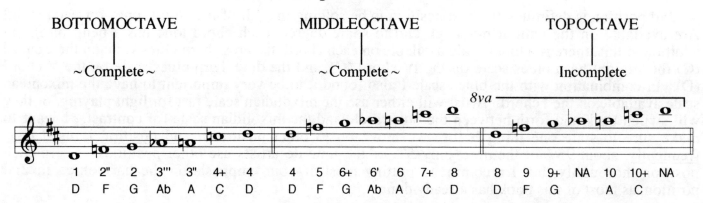

BOTTOM OCTAVE							MIDDLE OCTAVE							TOP OCTAVE						
~Complete~							~Complete~							Incomplete						
1	2"	2	3'''	3"	4+	4	4	5	6+	6'	6	7+	8	8	9	9+	NA	10	10+	NA
D	F	G	Ab	A	C	D	D	F	G	Ab	A	C	D	D	F	G		A	C	

50

#5) Is the mixolidian scale available on **I** chord? *The bottom octave is complete, the middle octave is missing the major third, and the top octave basically has two notes missing.*

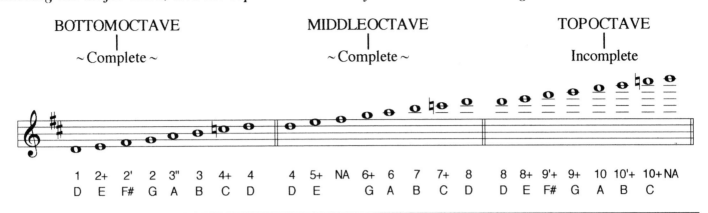

		BOTTOM OCTAVE							MIDDLE OCTAVE							TOP OCTAVE						

#1) Are the **IV** chord and **V** chord available? *Yes*
#2) Are the **IV** chord and **V** chord available on the harmonica's natural pitch set? *Yes, but the major third on the V chord is only available through articulate bending, so I opted to use the minor V.*

IV CHORD

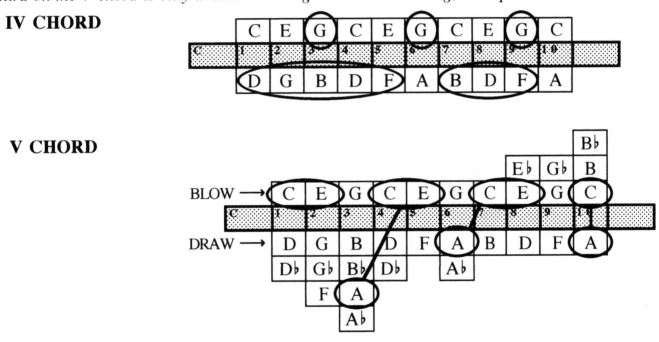

V CHORD

#3) Are there bends available on the **IV** chord and **V** chord? *The **IV** chord is very workable, but the **V** chord is barren of bends, and again, the third is lowered.*

IV CHORD

Yes

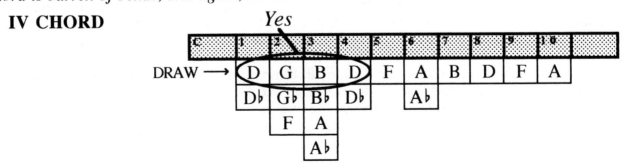

V CHORD

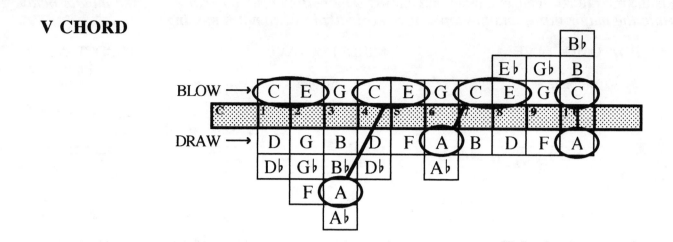

#4) Is there a blues scale available on the **V** chord? *Yes, but scarce.*

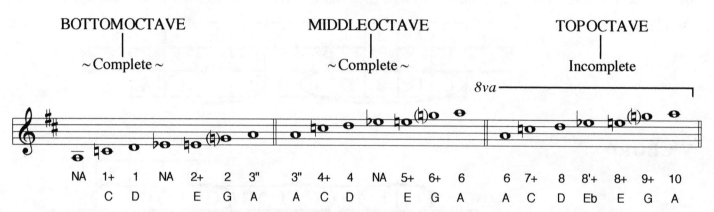

3rd Position Generalizations

Overall, 3rd position is one of the three most usable positions. Before we talk about the **I** chord, lets get the **IV** chord and **V** chord out of the way. The **IV** chord is based off of G, the same as the **I** chord in 2nd position. Even though the **IV** chord is usually replaced by **I** chord type soloing, it's a good idea to take advantage of the power packed cross harp blues scale for the **IV** chord in 3rd position. The **V** chord gets even more difficult to solo upon. The lack of bends on the chord itself makes playing very hard. Let's now talk about the **I** chord in 3rd position for a minute. As for having chord tones on the natural pitch set, 3rd position is most workable between the 4 draw and 10 draw. The only real problem we run into is where there should be F# there is only F-natural available to us on our C harmonica. This is both a help and a problem at the same time. Having the third lowered makes the blues scale easier to play, but when playing the flat-3 (as talked about in chapter 10 "techniques for bluesier playing: 'quarter tones'") it's normally played a little higher than the true flat for a bluesier sound. The answer is to use 3rd position mostly for playing blues in minor, and very dark blues. Because of the difficulty of constructing the mixolidian scale, 3rd position is more known for being a blues scale oriented position. Even with the drawbacks of 3rd position it's still a great position to solo in. As we play and study 3rd position together in this chapter notice the soloistic possibilities that 3rd position make available to us.

Generalizing Positions

After 3rd position a couple things start happening. As the number of flats or sharps increase, we must increasingly rely on bending to make the chord tones available. This starts eliminating: octaves, the warm sound of an open reed vibrating, and among other things the availability of bends lower than the chord tones. As we go past third position there are positions that have the blues scale available, but the difficulty of retrieving these blues scales are not usually worth the effort. The example below, based around the key of A with three sharps, demonstrates how sharps are negated when soloing strictly upon the blues scale.

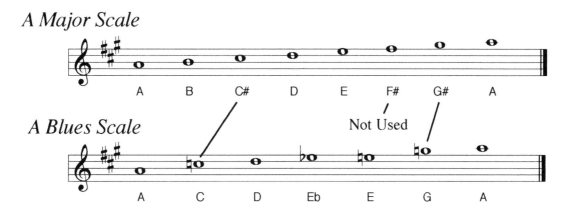

A Major Scale

A   B   C#   D   E   F#   G#   A

A Blues Scale

Not Used

A   C   D   Eb   E   G   A

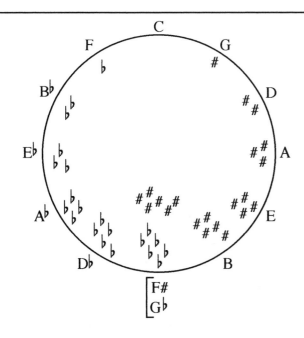

As you can see, the C#, F#, and G# that would normally take massive bending to retrieve are not needed when soloing strictly within the blues scale. When experimenting with other positions for yourself, follow the criteria checklist and see if the position holds up. One of the toughest things to understand about positions is their key relation to the original harmonica. The easiest and quickest way to find what key you are playing in is to count around the circle of fifths starting with the key of harmonica in which you are playing. If you have a G harmonica, start with your finger on G. G is 1st position; the next key to the right (D) is your key for 2nd position; the next key to the right of D is A; this is your key for 3rd, etc. If you want to go heavier into the study of positions I recommend my book through Mel Bay Publications called *Building Harmonica Technique*. *Building Harmonica Technique* goes into greater detail about soloing concepts than this book does.

Soloing In 3rd position

As just stated, 3rd position is based around the key of D on a C harmonica. The blues scale that is used on the **I** chord in 3rd position is called the draw harp blues scale. Take notice that this blues scale based off of D can also be used on the **V** chord in 2nd position, which is also based around D on a C harmonica. Written on the next page is the draw harp blues scale.

Octave Placement For Draw Harp

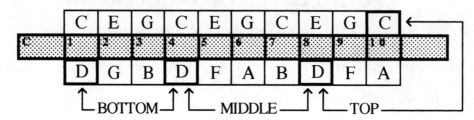

Draw Harp Blues Scales

I said before that the cross harp blues scale was the most usable blues scale on our harmonica, but the draw harp blues scale is the most complete. Both lower and middle octaves are complete. The middle octave is the most often used when soloing in 3rd position. Because of the articulate bending in the bottom octave of the blues scale it is used more sparingly. The upper octave works well for high runs and especially well when used in octaves. Looking at the diagram above, notice that you can get pure octaves on the **I** chord between the 8 draw and 10 draw (4/8, 5/9, 6/10). F, relative to the key of D, is the flat-3; what this makes available to us is a nice bluesy sounding run in octaves on the high end. The demonstration below, and 12 bar jam 11B, shows how these octaves can be used. As we did with all of the other positions, let's find the chord tones and root notes on the **I, IV,** and **V** in 3rd position.

5 Hole Octaves In 3rd Position

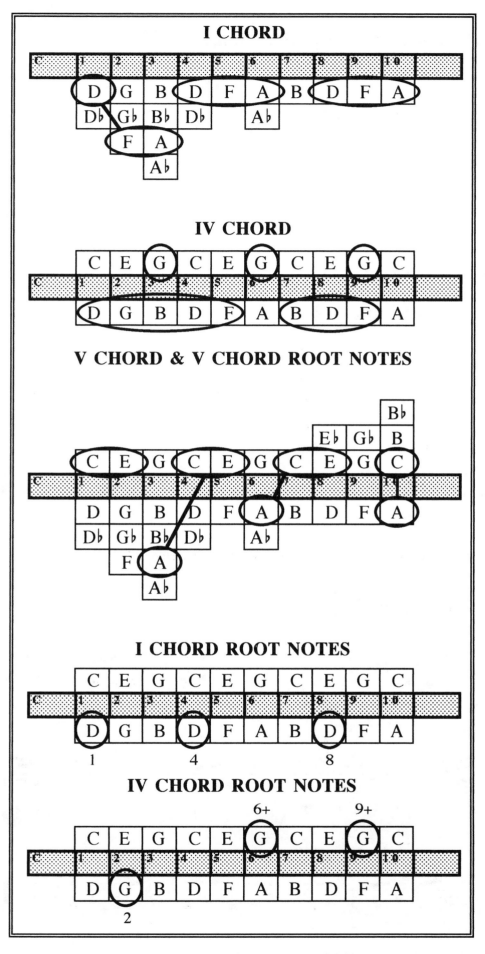

3rd Position Chords

The **I** chord relative to D is D - F# - A or D - F - A; the **IV** chord relative to D is G - B - D, the **V** chord relative to D is A - C# - E or A - C - E.

3rd Position Root Notes

The **I** chord root note is D and is found on the 1 draw, 4 draw, and 8 draw. The **I** chord root notes can also be played in a 1/4 or 4/8 octave. The **IV** chord root note is G and is found on the 2 draw, 6 blow, and 9 blow. The **IV** chord root notes can also be played in a 3+/6+ or 6+/9+ octave. The **V** chord root note is A and is found on 3 draw whole step bend, 6 draw, and 10 draw. The **V** chord root notes can also be played in a 6/10 octave. Written on the next page are two exercises to help you get used to 3rd position root notes.

3rd Position 12 Bar Blues Root Notes
Exercise 1

Exercise 2

12 Bar Jam 11A

12 Bar Jam 11B

30

I   All notes sound one octave higher than written

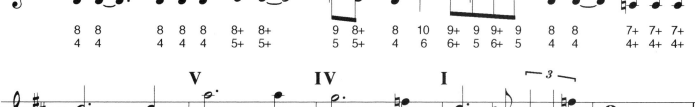

12 Bar Jam 11C

31

CLASSIC CHICAGO BLUES SONGS

I'm Ready
By Willie Dixon

 32

C Harmonica in 3rd Position

Solo Written by David Barrett

HOHNER'S OLD STANDBY #34-B
Photo Courtesy of Hohner Harmonicas

Chapter 14

SECTION 2 REVIEW

1) Write the cross harp scale from the 2 draw to the 6 blow using:

Hole Numbers -

				5	

Note Names -

				F	

2) Write the cross harp <u>blues</u> scale from the 2 draw to the 6 blow using:

Hole Numbers -

2						

Note Names -

G						

3) Octaves are used to send a _____ presentation of _____ note.

4) How many blow octaves are available? _____.

5) How many pure 4 hole embouchure octaves are available on the draw side? _____.

6) How many pure 5 hole embouchure octaves are available on the draw side? _____.

7) Fill in the blanks with the proper notes on the harmonica diagram below from memory.

BLOW →

C	1	2	3	4	5	6	7	8	9	10	

DRAW →

8) Take the two exercises below and transpose them to the high end.
   a) 6+, 5, 4, 5, 4, 4+, 3, 2   _ _ _ _ _ _ _ _
   b) 4, 5, 4, 5, 6+   _ _ _ _ _

9) Transpose the lick below to the low end.
   a) 6+, 7, 8, 8+, 9+, 9+   _ _ _ _ _ _

10) The term 1st position is used to say that you are (CH 4)_____

_____

11) The first note of a chord is called the _____.

12) Fill in the blanks with the proper notes on the harmonica diagram below; then, relative to <u>1st</u> position, circle the root notes for the **I, IV**, and **V** chord, labeling them accordingly.

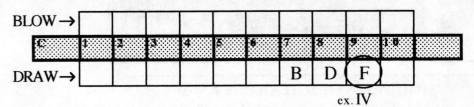

ex. IV

CHAPTER REVIEW ANSWERS

CHAPTER 2 REVIEW ANSWERS   **From Classic Chicago Blues Harp # 1**

1) The first way of looking at the harmonica's pitch set is to look at it as being <u>CHORDAL</u>.
2) The second way of looking at the harmonica's pitch set is to look at it as being based around the <u>MAJOR</u> <u>SCALE</u>.
3) The third way of looking at the harmonica's pitch set is by looking at its <u>OCTAVE</u> Placement.
4) Fill in the blanks with the proper notes on the harmonica diagram below.

BLOW →
C	E	G	C	E	G	C	E	G	C
C	1	2	3	4	5	6	7	8	9	10

DRAW →
D	G	B	D	F	A	B	D	F	A

CHAPTER 3 REVIEW ANSWERS   **From Classic Chicago Blues Harp # 1**

1) There are <u>FOUR</u> beats per measure, or bar in 4/4 time.
2) The number of beats a note receives determines the <u>DURATION</u> of a note.
3) The type of articulation you use determines the <u>ATTACK</u> of a note.
4) What were the three types of articulation mentioned? (list from strongest to softest attack) <u>TA</u>, <u>GA</u>, <u>HA</u>.
5) A whole note and whole rest each receive <u>FOUR</u> beats.
6) A half note and half rest each receive <u>TWO</u> beats.
7) A quarter note and quarter rest each receive <u>ONE QUARTER (1/4)</u> of a measure.
8) An eighth note and eighth rest each receive <u>ONE EIGHTH (1/8)</u> of a measure.
9) A sixteenth note and sixteenth rest each receive <u>ONE SIXTEENTH (1/16)</u> of a measure.
10) <u>THREE</u> triplets equal one beat.
11) The type of rhythmic feel blues uses is called <u>SWING</u>.
12) A tie combines the <u>DURATION</u> of two notes.
13) A dot, notated to the right of a note head, extends its value by <u>HALF</u>.
14) Fill in the blanks with the proper notes on the harmonica diagram below from memory.

BLOW →
C	E	G	C	E	G	C	E	G	C
C	1	2	3	4	5	6	7	8	9	10

DRAW →
D	G	B	D	F	A	B	D	F	A

CHAPTER 4 REVIEW ANSWERS   From Classic Chicago Blues Harp # 1

1) The term 1st position is used to say that you are <u>PLAYING IN THE KEY TO WHICH THE HARMONICA IS TUNED</u>.

2) The note from which a key is named, or the first scale degree of a scale is called your <u>TONIC</u>.

3) Place the proper chord symbols (roman numerals) above each bar of the blues progression.

I	I	I	I	IV	IV
I	I	V	IV	I	V/I

4) The first note of a chord is called the <u>ROOT NOTE</u>.

5) Fill in the blanks with the proper notes on the harmonica diagram below, then circle the root notes for the **I**, **IV**, and **V** chord labeling them accordingly.

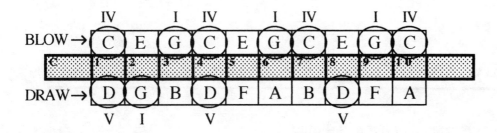

CHAPTER 5 REVIEW ANSWERS   From Classic Chicago Blues Harp # 1

1) One <u>QUESTION</u> and one <u>ANSWER</u> makes for one phrase.

2) There are many types of phrasing used within blues, but two prototypical types of phrasing are almost always used, the **V-IV-I** transition and the turnaround. Place the proper chord symbols (roman numerals) above each bar of the blues progression, then indicate where the **V-IV-I** transition and the turnaround is located.   <u>REFER TO PAGE 41</u>

3) A two hole shake is always started on the <u>BOTTOM</u> note.

4) Fill in the blanks with the proper notes on the harmonica diagram below, then circle the root notes for the **I**, **IV**, and **V** chord, labeling them accordingly.

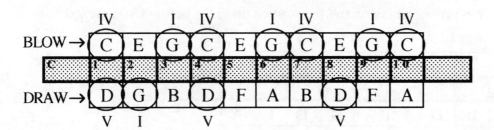

CHAPTER 6 REVIEW ANSWERS

From Classic Chicago Blues Harp # 1

1) The smallest distance you can have between two notes in the major scale is the <u>HALF</u> <u>STEP</u>.

2) Fill in the bend chart below.

Bend Chart

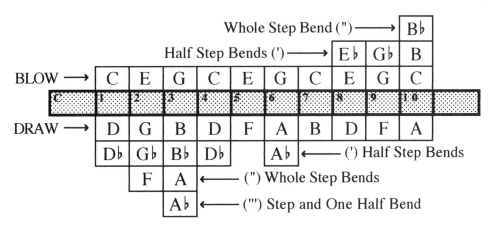

3) Fill in the blanks with the proper notes on the harmonica diagram below, then circle the root notes for the **I, IV**, and **V** chord, labeling them accordingly.

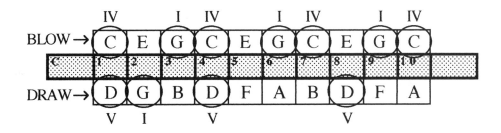

From Classic Chicago Blues Harp # 1

SECTION 1 REVIEW ANSWERS

1) The number of beats a note receives determines the <u>DURATION</u> of a note.

2) The type of articulation you use determines the <u>ATTACK</u> of a note.

3) What were the three types of articulation mentioned? (list from strongest to softest attack)
<u>TA</u>, <u>GA</u>, <u>HA</u>.

4) The type of rhythmic feel blues uses is called <u>SWING</u>.

5) A tie combines the <u>DURATION</u> of two notes.

6) A dot, notated to the right of a note head, extends its value by <u>HALF</u>.

7) The term 1st position is used to say that you are <u>PLAYING IN THE KEY TO WHICH THE HARMONICA IS TUNED</u>.

8) The note from which a key is named, or the first scale degree of a scale is called your <u>TONIC</u>.

9) The first note of a chord is called the <u>ROOT NOTE</u>.

10) Fill in the blanks with the proper notes on the harmonica diagram below, then circle the root notes for the **I**, **IV**, and **V** chord labeling them accordingly.

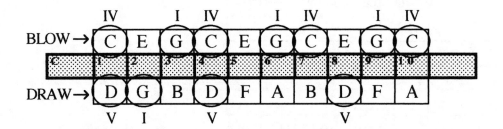

11) Place the proper chord symbols (roman numerals) above each bar of the blues progression.

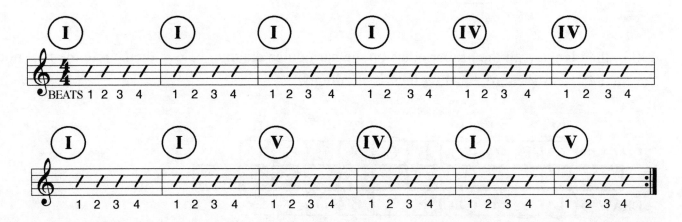

12) Analyze the example below from page 61, appropriately notating with brackets where these following techniques occur:

A) Each Question   C) Each Statement   E) V-IV-I Transition

B) Each Answer   D) Each Phrase   F) Turnaround

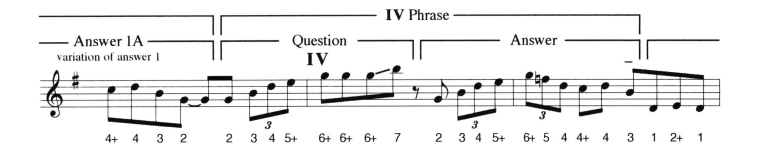

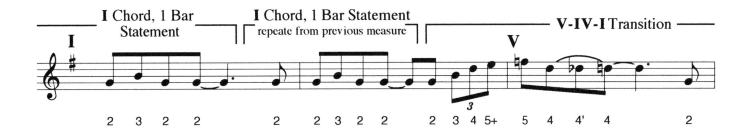

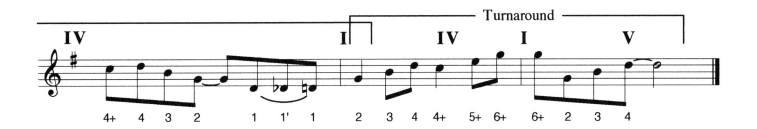

13) Fill in the bend chart below.

Bend Chart

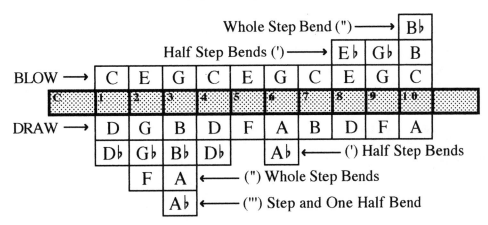

CHAPTER 10 REVIEW

1) The objective in playing in 2nd position is to make our <u>ONE</u> <u>CHORD</u> on the draw side so all the blue notes and bends are available to us at will.

2) 2nd position on our C harmonica is based around the key of <u>G</u>.

3) Write each note found in the three chords used in blues relative to G:

   I chord <u>G B D</u>   **IV** chord <u>C E G</u>   **V** chord <u>D F A</u>

4) Write the <u>notes</u> (not hole numbers) found in the G major scale:

G	A	B	C	D	E	F#	G

5) Write the cross harp scale from the 2 draw to the 6 blow using:

   Hole Numbers -

2	3	4+	4	5	6+

   Note Names -

G	B	C	D	F	G

6) Write the cross harp <u>blues</u> scale from the 2 draw to the 6 blow using:

   Hole Numbers -

2	3'	4+	4'	4	5	6+

   Note Names -

G	Bb	C	Db	D	F	G

SECTION 2 REVIEW ANSWERS

1) Write the cross harp scale from the 2 draw to the 6 blow using:

   Hole Numbers -

2	3	4+	4	5	6+

   Note Names -

G	B	C	D	F	G

2) Write the cross harp <u>blues</u> scale from the 2 draw to the 6 blow using:

   Hole Numbers -

2	3'	4+	4'	4	5	6+

   Note Names -

G	Bb	C	Db	D	F	G

3) Octaves are used to send a <u>BROADER</u> presentation of <u>ONE</u> note.

4) How many blow octaves are available? <u>7</u>.

5) How many pure 4 hole embouchure octaves are available on the draw side? <u>1</u>.

6) How many pure 5 hole embouchure octaves are available on the draw side? <u>4</u>.

7) Fill in the blanks with the proper notes on the harmonica diagram below from memory.

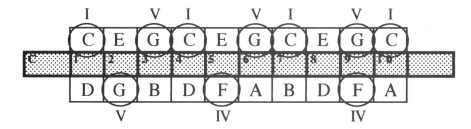

BLOW → | C | E | G | C | E | G | C | E | G | C |

DRAW → | D | G | B | D | F | A | B | D | F | A |

8) Take the two exercises below and transpose them to the high end.

    a) 6+, 5, 4, 5, 4, 4+, 3, 2   9+, 9, 8, 9, 8 7+, 7, 6+

    b) 4, 5, 4, 5, 6+   8, 9, 8, 9, 9+

9) Transpose the lick below to the low end.

    a) 6+, 7, 8, 8+, 9+, 9+   2, 3, 4, 5+, 6+, 6+

10) The term 1st position is used to say that you are (CH 4) <u>PLAYING IN THE KEY THE HARMONICA IS TUNED TO.</u>

11) The first note of a chord is called the <u>ROOT</u>.

12) Fill in the blanks with the proper notes on the harmonica diagram below; then, relative to <u>1st position</u>, circle the root notes for the **I**, **IV**, and **V** chord labeling them accordingly.

Somber Howlin' Wolf   *Photo By Scott Shigley*

Harmonica Position Chart

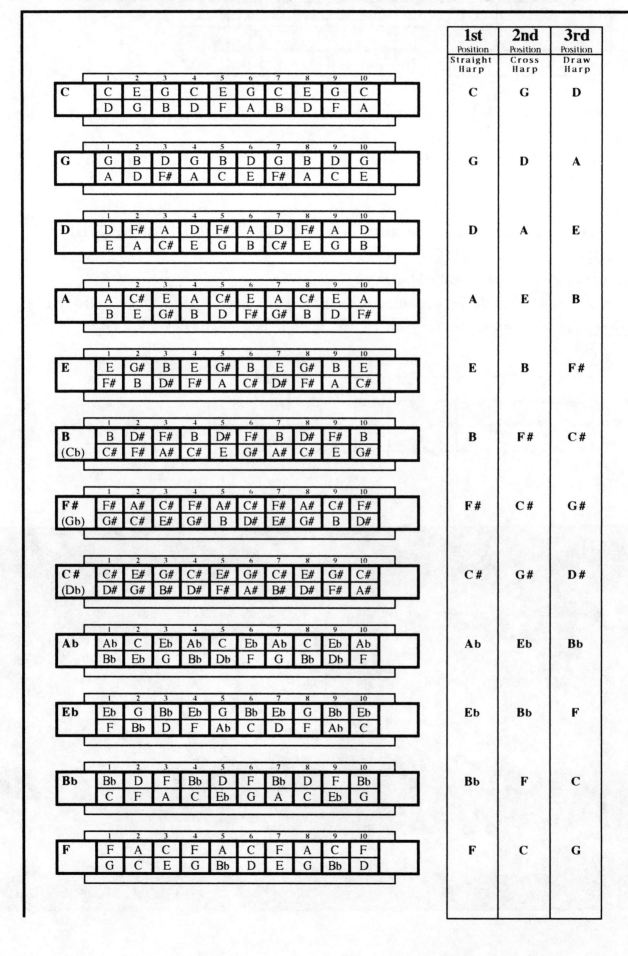

												1st Position Straight Harp	2nd Position Cross Harp	3rd Position Draw Harp
C	C	E	G	C	E	G	C	E	G	C		C	G	D
	D	G	B	D	F	A	B	D	F	A				
G	G	B	D	G	B	D	G	B	D	G		G	D	A
	A	D	F#	A	C	E	F#	A	C	E				
D	D	F#	A	D	F#	A	D	F#	A	D		D	A	E
	E	A	C#	E	G	B	C#	E	G	B				
A	A	C#	E	A	C#	E	A	C#	E	A		A	E	B
	B	E	G#	B	D	F#	G#	B	D	F#				
E	E	G#	B	E	G#	B	E	G#	B	E		E	B	F#
	F#	B	D#	F#	A	C#	D#	F#	A	C#				
B (Cb)	B	D#	F#	B	D#	F#	B	D#	F#	B		B	F#	C#
	C#	F#	A#	C#	E	G#	A#	C#	E	G#				
F# (Gb)	F#	A#	C#	F#	A#	C#	F#	A#	C#	F#		F#	C#	G#
	G#	C#	E#	G#	B	D#	E#	G#	B	D#				
C# (Db)	C#	E#	G#	C#	E#	G#	C#	E#	G#	C#		C#	G#	D#
	D#	G#	B#	D#	F#	A#	B#	D#	F#	A#				
Ab	Ab	C	Eb	Ab	C	Eb	Ab	C	Eb	Ab		Ab	Eb	Bb
	Bb	Eb	G	Bb	Db	F	G	Bb	Db	F				
Eb	Eb	G	Bb	Eb	G	Bb	Eb	G	Bb	Eb		Eb	Bb	F
	F	Bb	D	F	Ab	C	D	F	Ab	C				
Bb	Bb	D	F	Bb	D	F	Bb	D	F	Bb		Bb	F	C
	C	F	A	C	Eb	G	A	C	Eb	G				
F	F	A	C	F	A	C	F	A	C	F		F	C	G
	G	C	E	G	Bb	D	E	G	Bb	D